INTRODUCTION

Life to the full?

If the current spirituality craze is to be believed, the answer to our often stress-filled, chaotic, empty lives, is actually quite simple: colouring books.

They are all the rage. In cafes, parks and office canteens across the western world, grown adults can be found serenely colouring-in anything from tawny owls and exotic flowers to cute teddy bears.

One such book, called *Peace, Calm and Colouring,* boasts of helping to 'achieve your goal of inner peace' and 'clear your mind of any worries or anxieties'. If only spiritual fulfilment was that simple!

What's interesting about these modern mindfulness techniques is the importance of **emptying** yourself, in order to feel better inside. Not so with the Christian faith, though. Our chief pursuit is **fullness** - in all its pain and glory.

'I have come so that they may have life, and have it to the full', says Jesus Christ, in what is surely one of the most quoted verses in the entire Gospels. It's his promise to abundantly fill our lives. To satisfy our inner yearnings. To quench our thirst. To make us whole. The lives of Christ's followers are supposed to be full. And yet - if we're honest - many of us so often feel anything but. We are running on empty at home, at work, at play and, yes, at church. In practice this 'full life' remains maddeningly elusive.

Over these four sessions we're going to explore what it might mean to actually experience this fullness in the midst of our messy lives. What does it look like? Why does it seem so elusive? What causes us to run on empty? And, maybe, how could we help others to experience this fullness?

To help us on our journey, I'll be using four reference points from the world of TV, literature, poetry and rock music as our spiritual muse.

We won't need paints or crayons in these sessions - just an eagerness to 'colour-in' with our honest discussions, stories, reflections and prayer. So often our Christian lives become shaded with greys and blacks. Perhaps we can use this course to daub some dazzling new colours on our spiritual landscape?

As we do that, we can pray that a new sense of Christ's fullness might be illuminated within us.

> "I am daily amazed by the fact that God loves me. And that's something that inspires gratitude and joy. I can't … I *can* believe it … I *do* believe it. I do believe it. But in a sense it's almost unbelievable - it's overwhelming. There's so much that I can give thanks for."
>
> *Archbishop Justin Welby*

Session 1: Hummingbird or Arctic Fox?

Read John 10.1-15

Let me begin with a confession. I committed a cardinal sin recently, a thing that no loving son or daughter should ever do. It was too terrible for words. I covered myself in sackcloth and ashes for days afterwards.

My mum had called me for a chat. The end of the phone conversation went something like this:

Me: "So, what are you doing for the rest of the day, Mum?"

Mum: "I'm being taken out for a nice meal."

Me: "That's nice. What's the occasion?"

Mum: "It's my birthday."

NO! I forgot my own precious mother's birthday! The truck-load of flowers and chocolate I quickly sent her were a desperate way to atone for my sin. But I still felt terrible. I was too preoccupied. Too busy tearing around all over the place. Too wrapped up in the frenzy of what I was doing to leave room in my head to remember such an important date. I'd fallen foul of what I call 'the hummingbird life' yet again. Most of us are not immune to it.

In this first session we'll look at what a hummingbird life is and see how it can apply to our faith, especially what it means in the context of living more fully. And then we'll discover that the feeding habits of the arctic fox might provide some better answers...

Life in all its fullness

But first, I've always been a keen student of what Jesus actually meant by living 'life in all its fullness' (John 10.10). When I was nibbling at the edges of faith, this promise was one of the reasons I went for it in the end. It seemed like very good news to me. The question is: if the fullest kind of life is what Jesus intended for his followers, how do we get access to it? What might it look and feel like in the midst of our ordinary lives?

I recently saw an Oscar Wilde quote that stopped me in my tracks. He wrote: *'To live is the rarest thing in the world. Most people just exist.'* The way many of us 'do' life, faith and, yes, even church, in the maelstrom of modern society would seem to suggest he had a point.

And yet Jesus Christ - in his promise of full living - offers a radical

> "We work to become, not to acquire."
>
> *Elbert Hubbard, author*

alternative to jus ... challenges us to ... about the way w... A choice that ha... profoundly imp... our existence ar... out our Christian faith in the world. what we think and experience inwardly; how we come across to those around us; how we treat others. Whether we feel like we are just existing, or fully living right now, it must be worth exploring.

Harassed and helplesss

One of the most moving moments in the entire Gospels is when Jesus looks upon the crowd in Matthew 9.36. It says that he was filled with compassion *'because they were harassed and helpless, like sheep without a shepherd.'* How reassuring that God looks upon his flawed, messy creation in this way. This rushing, crushing crowd appears lost in the chaos and struggle of their lives. Jesus is staring out at emptiness in all its human form - the good shepherd sent to provide an answer to that way of living. With compassion, peace and transforming love, his invitation and message to them was simple, but potentially life-transforming: come and be filled.

What was true then is of course true now. Many of us can identify with that crowd. We exist with that same harassed helplessness. We fight emptiness all our lives. It comes in a myriad of forms. It strikes at different times: struggles with fear, ...ety, self-doubt, identity - ... is that prevents us from ...people God intends us

...ion and following

I beca... a Christian one night in my late (troubled!) teens. I ran downstairs to excitedly announce the world-changing news to my older sister. She looked over at me - in that special withering way only older sisters can do - and said: "I give it two weeks, Matt. Now get lost. I'm watching *EastEnders*!"

It did last, though. Since then I've tried, and failed many times, to take Jesus at his word - to reject the idea of mere existence; to relentlessly pursue this ideal of full Christian living.

Results have been mixed on occasion. Like when I tried to demonstrate to hundreds of visiting school children at my old church that being a Jesus follower could be full not dull. In hindsight, climbing out of the towering pulpit to make this point while our organist played the *Mission Impossible* theme tune was a terrible idea. I was left dangling over the edge, clinging on for dear

> "Addiction to the brilliant new technologies is becoming endemic. Theologically speaking, any addiction that displaces God in the inner habitation of the soul needs to be rooted out."
>
> *Ron Ferguson Church of Scotland minister*

life. I nearly killed myself - and the Lord Mayor of Hull below me. They didn't forget that sermon in a hurry.

Goals and gates

One of the great joys of wearing a dog collar for a living is the regular opportunity it gives me to explore faith with all manner of people.

I've done lots of Christian basics courses over the years. We always start with a discussion about what's most important to us in life. My groups list their top ten life goals. Interestingly, the top answers are nearly always heart and soul aspirations rather than physical or material desires. Things like, 'inner peace', 'true joy' and 'healthy relationships'. The new Volvo, dream holiday to Disney World and romantic liaison with Tom Cruise on a Caribbean beach are always way down the list. It has taught me that most of us recognise an innate desire, deep within, to experience a full inner life beyond the trappings of the material world. Christ's bold claim in our John 10 passage is that he is the gate through which all that is possible.

I've learnt that people seem to walk through that gate in all manner of surprising ways. Tony is one such person. He began to explore faith after turning up to an alternative church service I ran in a tough city centre pub called The Mission (appropriate name!). Tony told me that night that he'd been on the verge of despair. His newborn son had been on a life support machine and given little chance of survival. One night in the hospital chapel Tony had prayed for the first time. "Dear God, please let Henry live!" he pleaded. "I promise to start going to church." A few days later, Henry got better. Tony said his heart sank when he remembered his divine deal. Then he noticed an article in the local paper. It reported on a new service for those who don't normally go to church, in a pub called The Mission. Its name was 'The Full Service'. Tony found faith - and fullness - in the end. Tony has since discovered, as many of us do, that living life in all its fullness is an ongoing journey. God certainly does work in mysterious ways.

Life Story - hummingbirds

The scourge of spiritual emptiness is always a clear and present danger. This was brought into sharp focus for me a few years ago, when I was sitting transfixed watching David Attenborough's stunning *Life Story* BBC TV nature series. It brought to life the habits, struggles and interactions of all manner of weird and wonderful wildlife.

> "I'm a Roman Catholic. One of the reasons I believe in God is because when I read the New Testament, I think it tells us how to live."
>
> *Baroness Shirley Williams*

> "Most people cannot be silent, or solitary, for long; and it is a full-time vocation for very few. But it is more than a necessary, if brief, escape from distractions so that grace can begin its work."
>
> Church Times *Comment*

One episode featured the booted racket-tail hummingbird and the arctic fox. I was immediately struck by what a starkly contrasting picture they painted of our own often schizophrenic spiritual lives. It was painful to watch. The hummingbird reminded me how so many of us interact with God and live out our faith. And I was struck by how God calls us to be arctic foxes.

The hummingbirds are in a constant high-speed race to feed on nectar. These tiny birds need a hit of the stuff 2,000 times a day in order to survive. They dart from flower to flower frantically sucking it up. It was exhausting viewing - like watching my twin daughters attacking their McDonald's milkshakes. The hummingbirds literally don't have time for anything else. They collapse exhausted into their nests at night. The feeding frenzy starts again at first light. Their lives are a super-fast treadmill simply to exist.

This sounded familiar. Stressed home environments, busy shopping streets, station platforms, school drop offs and manic priests forgetting their mother's birthday ... I think we see the harassed and helpless hummingbird life all around us. Too many of us are hummingbird Christians, sucking up fleeting hits of the God nectar before we rush on to the next thing. Emptying ourselves in the process.

Life story - arctic fox

David Attenborough then turned his attention to the arctic fox. What a contrast. These beautiful animals exist in the harshest snowiest conditions. Food is scarce. The fox must be slow, quiet and alert in order to survive. It listens for signs of movement and life under the snow. Ears craning against the snow, it stops. It waits. It listens. When it hears the faintest movement, it leaps into the air and dives headfirst. The fox's head disappears deep down into the ice and snow in the hope of catching its prey. One feed can fill the fox for days before it has to go searching under the surface once again.

Some of us are natural foxes: slow, careful, measured listeners. Others, like me, are hardwired hummingbirds. Fast and darting. Rushed, stressed and busy. In the context of our spiritual lives, though, I think God is calling us to the snowy feeding grounds. To the spiritual sustenance beneath the surface. I've found that's where the most satisfying food is.

Our challenge is to stop rushing. To make time to listen. To sense where God is, where his Spirit is moving. Where he's leading us to find that sense of calling and nourishment.

> "One of the most time-consuming things is to have an enemy."
>
> *E B White, writer*

And then to be unafraid to leap and go in deep. I think this might be one of the keys to experiencing - and living out - this full life that Jesus speaks of. Going deeper. It's simple, obvious and we hear it all the time in church.

And yet so many of us remain trapped in our hummingbird life. No more so than in the season of Advent. A time set aside to wait, ponder and reflect on the Christ child, but a time that so often sees us flit and fly from one thing to the next - sucking up the nectar of gifts to buy; food to consume and family commitments to honour.

It was interesting to watch how many times the arctic fox bashes his nose as he mistimes a dive. Or the occasions when he overdoes it, and his head gets stuck in the snow. Finding the time, the space and the energy to go deeper with God, to hear his voice in the quiet, is far from easy. In the end though, the fox perseveres and prevails. It can be the same for us.

Going deeper

St John of the Cross knew about the way of the arctic fox. He wrote that *'the thicket of God's wisdom and knowledge is so deep and so broad that the soul, however much it has come to know of it, can always penetrate deeper within it.'* Fullness in Christ means finding time and space to go deeper. To really focus and feed. It makes a massive difference. We often mistakenly believe that our faith is not robust enough, our lives are not 'holy' enough and our prayers are not spiritual enough to give us deeper access to Christ's fullness. I believed that for a long time - until two nuns taught me different.

My late spiritual director Sister Cecilia Goodman was one. I came out in a cold sweat in our first session. Sharing doubts and fears with a real-life nun! She was as well spoken as the Queen Mother and had more God books than a university library. I quickly realised though, that she was as 'normal' and broken as the rest of us piling into her room for spiritual guidance. She taught me that our callings, circumstances and pronunciation might be different - but that life in all its fullness is open to every one of Christ's followers. Including me. Including you.

Cecilia encouraged people to burrow deeply into the snow through a combination of honest reflection and Ignatian spirituality. In my case

> "Silence is held in great esteem by spiritual people of all religions, and it is much more than the absence of sound. It is a precious means of access into the spiritual world."
>
> *Cardinal Cormac Murphy-O'Conor*

that meant learning to be still, keep my mouth shut for an hour and use the silence to imagine Christ with me in the midst of my ordinary life. I plumbed new depths with him. I left the convent fed, restored and just a little bit fuller. These techniques are not just reserved for nunneries though. Hillsides, basements, quiet cafe corners - Arctic fox moments can be experienced pretty much anywhere.

From existing to living

Cecilia also urged me to read *Sister Wendy On Prayer*. The writings of this hermit nun with the serious art history habit (sorry!) revolutionised my approach to prayer. Get it if you can. She encourages us to simply give God what we've got and who we are - warts and all - and He will do the rest.

Sister Wendy writes: *'Perhaps you have a baby? Perhaps you have an especially demanding workload? Perhaps you are lonely? Perhaps you are angry? None of this matters. It is who you are that God comes to in prayer, and if it is a tired, fractious, despondent man or woman, He still takes you to Himself with infinite love and makes the best of what you can give Him.'*

Abraham Lincoln said that, *'In the end it's not the years in your life that count. It's the life in your years.'* I'd want to add that it's the Jesus-shaped life in your years that count. With Jesus closer and deeper, they could be years that are fuller - bursting with new life. Lives with more joy, hope and peace in them. Let's not be people who just exist. Let's not be a church that just exists.

Feed on these inspiring words from Psalm 42: *'Deep calls to deep in the roar of your waterfalls; all your waves and breakers have swept over me. By day the Lord directs his love, at night his song is with me - a prayer to the God of my life.'*

May you seek depth and find fullness in the roar of your waterfalls, day by day.

"One of the classic definitions of prayer is 'the raising of the heart and mind to God'. How this happens in practice depends entirely on the individual, and has a great deal more to do with choice and perseverance than feeling. And it has everything to do with God and not with ourselves … We all have difficult days, and it is not unusual to start this [second hour of prayer at 5pm] fuming, with the world, with individuals and with oneself and with God. It is advisable to give this state of affairs to God, however nasty a present it may seem. By the end of the hour one is often in a far better frame of mind without knowing how this has happened."

Sister Teresa, columnist and Carmelite nun

Questions for Groups

YOU DON'T HAVE TO ANSWER ALL THE QUESTIONS!!

You can use some of your own if you prefer.

You should find that most of the questions refer to something either in the course booklet or on the audio (CD or download).

1. Matt Woodcock forgot his mum's birthday! What's the worst thing that you've ever forgotten?
2. **Read John 10.10:** What do you think 'life in all its fullness' or 'to have life abundantly' might mean in today's world?
3. **Track 4 of the audio/transcript:** Could you share a time in your life when you felt spiritually empty?
4. **Re-read Oscar Wilde's quote on p. 2:** Do you agree with him?
5. **Re-visit 'Conversion and following' on p. 3:** Have you ever talked to anyone about your faith? If so, what was the reaction?
6. **Re-visit Tony's faith story on p. 4:** What's your reaction? Do you have a faith story to share?
7. **Re-visit 'Going deeper' on p. 6 and track 6:** Does anything prevent you from 'going deeper' with God?
8. **Track 7:** Are you a hummingbird or an arctic fox? In what ways does your Christian journey resemble these animals?
9. **Re-read Sister Wendy's words on prayer on p. 7 and track 9:** How do you cope with or use prayer?
10. **Re-read the words from Psalm 42 on p. 7:** How will you 'seek depth and find fullness in the roar of your waterfalls' this week?

"Within religion hope was prized highly. Of faith, hope and charity, it was hope that bound us together in a belief in the afterlife, allowing us to transcend our immediate situation, believe in God's will and look to a future of promise and possibilities. Without hope, whole cultures would have been sunk. On a personal level, hope is good for us. High-hopers procrastinate less, can withstand discomfort and pain more (twice as much, studies prove) and are less anxious and have fewer depressive symptoms than their less hopeful peers."

Tanis Taylor, writer

Session 2: Murdstone or Peggotty?

Read: John 12.1-8

Far too often I'm the loudest person in the room. Just ask my wife - I embarrass her constantly. I've always had a natural propensity to interact with people at great volume. I'd make a terrible librarian. At school it was the same. It often got me into trouble. In one science lesson an elderly supply teacher called Mr Goldhammer shouted so loudly at me to be quiet that his false teeth flew out of his mouth and clattered across the classroom!

There's a danger you could think that 'life in all its fullness' is reserved for raving extroverts like me. The very word 'full' has a loud and proud feeling to it somehow. In reality, though, Christ offers this way of living to everyone: the introverts and extroverts, the rough and refined, the confident and timid. Or, in worship terms, whether you prefer a quiet, candlelit side chapel playing soothing Taizé music, or bouncing up and down with arms aloft in front of a hirsute Christian rock metal band.

Nevertheless, as we continue to explore living life to the full, it's worth reflecting on whether there are key characteristics, common threads and distinctive traits associated with this way of being. The nine fruits of the Spirit from Galatians 5: love, joy, peace, patience, kindness, generosity, faithfulness, gentleness and self-control offer a helpful template of the sort of qualities that emerge from someone living in the fullness of Christ.

More generally though, I think we often instinctively know when we're in the company of a 'full' person. There's just a distinctive Christ-like cut to their jib in their way with God, faith and other people. There's an openness to them. A special warmth and compassion. An infectious joy.

In John 15.10-11, Jesus compels his followers to: *'Remain in my love … so that my joy may be in you, and that your joy may be complete.'* Of course, when that joy is not complete, when we extract ourselves from the love of Christ and live out of our own emptiness, our faith journey can take on a different hue. Dark shadows can loom over ourselves, the people around us, and the churches we worship in.

> "These days loneliness is the new cancer – a shameful, embarrassing thing, brought upon yourself in some obscure way."
>
> *Gail Honeyman, writer*

Reflecting on the core ingredients of the full life, I was inspired by Charles Dickens' *David Copperfield.* Particular characters - the Murdstones and the Peggottys - resonated. They seemed to hold a mirror up to what we are so often like as followers of Christ - at our fullest and our emptiest.

Dickens and Jesus

Jesus Christ was important to Charles Dickens, who even wrote his own version of the Gospels to read to his children at bedtime. He called it *The Life of our Lord.* In the introduction, he writes: *'My dear children, I am very anxious that you should know something about the History of Jesus Christ. For everybody ought to know about Him. No one ever lived who was so good, so kind, so gentle, and so sorry for all the people who did wrong, or were in any way ill or miserable …'.*

Dickens appeared to know about what it meant to live in the fullness of Christ. He knew about living on empty too. I found *David Copperfield* to be a profoundly spiritual book. It puts flesh and bone onto the heart of the human condition. It refuses to sugarcoat or romanticise what life and people can be really like. It's us at our worst and our best – and no more so than with the Murdstones and the Peggottys. Two sets of siblings but polar opposites. Two ways of being. Grim and beautiful characters that paint a picture (albeit a rather exaggerated one) of what our faith can often look and feel like.

> "Of the seven deadly sins, only envy is no fun at all."
> *Joseph Epstein, writer*

David Copperfield is essentially about one boy's journey to maturity - from an impoverished and miserable childhood to becoming a successful and famous author. It is thought to draw from the early life of Dickens himself.

The Murdstones

The young Copperfield is forced to live with the Murdstone siblings after his gentle widowed mother marries Edward Murdstone, whose poisonous sister Jane (who'd make a great panto baddie) then moves in too.

The Murdstones are dark souls - sneering, mean-spirited, joyless, negative, and cold. At their worst, they are abusive and cruel. They revel in others' misfortunes and hoover the joy from any room they are in. It doesn't take them long to corrupt the joyful, warm atmosphere of the Copperfield household. David narrates his days as being filled with *'grievous daily drudgery and misery.'* It makes him *'sullen, dull and dogged.'* For his mother, her natural gaiety and beauty is *'worried away'* by the Murdstones' constant callous sniping.

When it comes to their brand of Christianity, Dickens' writes that, *'The gloomy taint that was in the Murdstone blood, darkened the Murdstone religion, which was austere and wrathful.'* Copperfield describes the *'dreaded Sunday'* coming round, and filing into an old pew *'like a guarded captive brought to a condemned service.'* I hope that's not your Sunday experience!

The Murdstones' warped attitude to life, faith and people reminded me what we can be like on our worst days. Those times when we descend into a cycle of negativity. When we harshly treat or judge others. When we snipe, sneer and gossip. When we think the worst, and never look for the best. And just like in the Copperfield's home, our gloomy pessimism can so easily infect those around us.

Murdstone types are like the Dementor characters in the Harry Potter books. They are creatures that *'drain peace, hope, and happiness out of the air around them ... Get too near a Dementor and every good feeling, every happy memory will be sucked out of you.'* (I'm firmly resisting a mother-in-law joke at this point.)

I suspect we can all admit to some Murdstone moments on occasion. It can be an unwelcome character trait of our Christian lives. I'm as guilty as anyone. After finishing university, stuck in a cycle of dead-end jobs, I went through an empty period of being resentful, bored and restless. Church was something I did begrudgingly. I was that bloke on the back pew on Sunday morning, moaning about how rubbish everything was. The sermon? Too boring. The worship? Too cheesy. The refreshments? Too much quiche. I was a walking rain cloud and drenched anyone who came near me. Thankfully it didn't last. Our youth worker reminded me what a follower of Christ was supposed to look like. The sun came back out.

> "It is easier to love humanity as a whole than it is to love one's neighbour."
> *Eric Hoffer, philosopher*

The Peggottys

Back to the pages of *David Copperfield*: Clara and Daniel Peggotty are 'fullness' personified. They are the yin to the Murdstones' yang. Relentlessly cheerful, fiercely loyal, generous, kind-hearted, and colourful. They shine love and light on any room they are in.

With *'cheeks like a red apple'*, Clara is the Copperfield's old nurse and housekeeper. The Murdstones' negative powers can't penetrate her armour of unwavering compassion and love. In one scene, she appears at the door that Copperfield has been locked behind for days. Through the keyhole she showers him with reassurance, encouragement and affection. It has a profound impact. He narrates: *'From that night there grew up in my breast a feeling for Peggotty which I cannot very well define ...she came into a vacancy in my heart, which closed upon her.'*

Clara's brother, Daniel, is a simple, poor fisherman. He lives in a converted boat with his adopted niece and nephew. It's a life of selfless devotion, natural warmth, hospitality, and generosity of spirit. He is filled with the milk of human kindness.

The Peggottys are Copperfield's 'Patronus charm'. In the Harry Potter books the Patronus charm is the only spell that can ward off a Dementor. It is the purest of light generated from a wizard's most positive feelings. In Christian terms, there's enormous spiritual power in a positive, joyful spirit. It gets to the heart of living out Christ's fullness.

Susie

My late friend Susie was a born Peggotty. She lived the full life - even though everything seemed stacked against her. Born with a defective spine, she was 3 feet 8 inches tall, weighed 4 stone and was confined to a wheelchair. Later in life she was blinded with a cigarette by an abusive boyfriend. She refused to descend into hopeless, bitter despair. Quite the opposite. Susie's heart and love for others, her desire to see everyone treated as equals, no matter what their disability, was inspirational.

Susie began a love affair with Jesus Christ after attending one of our Christmas carol services. She immediately wanted all her friends to know him too. Our services became filled with her karaoke pals. My pastoral load tripled in a week. She'd make me lift her out of the wheelchair and dance with her at the front when we played the gospel song *I Saw The Light*. At her funeral, I made sure everyone danced to it. Susie turned the hearts and minds of many a Murdstone.

Fullness in action

Mary's anointing of Jesus in our reading from John 12.1-8 brings a Gospel perspective to our reflections. It's an example of 'fullness' in action. We find Mary pouring generous amounts of expensive perfume onto the feet and hair of Jesus. It's an intimate, extravagant gesture - a moment of beautiful affection. It is a representation of the depth of love Mary feels for her Lord.

Verse 3 says the house is filled with the sweet fragrance. And then verse 4, beginning as it does with a *'but'*, reads like a wet fish slap across the face - a Murdstone enters the room: Judas Iscariot. He spoils the purity and joy of the encounter. Suddenly Mary's fragrant gesture is a problem to be solved, rather than a moment to enjoy. It's become a waste of resources. You can almost feel the perfume being wafted away with his negative chastisement.

> "It is said that, when Handel heard his Hallelujah Chorus for the first time, deeply moved he declared: 'I did see all Heaven open before my eyes.'"

It reminds me of a house party I threw once in my late teens when my parents went away. I transformed our front room into a nightclub. Low lighting. Soft music. Loads of friends. A slow dance with my latest teenage crush. The night was a triumph. That was until my older sister burst in. "MATTHEW - what on earth is going on?!" she bellowed. The lights went on. The music was cut. My dream girl scurried into the night with the rest of the guests. Party over.

In our Christian lives, it doesn't take much to pop the balloons on a Spirit-filled occasion. To sour a positive atmosphere. To pull people down rather than lift them up. To put the top back on the perfume bottle. Notice how Jesus confronts such attitudes in the Gospels. He can't abide them. Be it the judgemental chief priests, the hypocritical Pharisees, or his own mean-spirited disciples, Jesus challenges the Murdstones: "Leave her alone!" he commands Judas.

Peggotty-type churches

My current role is to travel all over the Diocese of York helping churches to grow. It's interesting what the flourishing Christian communities have in common. They are Peggotty-type churches. There's a distinctive culture of warmth, welcome, poignant worship, laughter, compassion, spiritual depth - and cracking good biscuits. Passing the Peace at Holy Communion in these churches seem to go on for days!

> "Why does God make us feel the questions if he doesn't give us any answers?"
>
> *From the Coen brothers' film* A Serious Man

A vicar friend of mine had his leaving service recently at a church where he'd overseen extraordinary growth. He was asked to share what had made the biggest difference. He listed three key changes:

1. making joy and laughter a normal, expected part of the Sunday worship

2. insisting on the church's front door being permanently left open

3. dishing out extravagant handfuls of huge chocolate buttons to the children who came up to the rail at Holy Communion

What a picture of fullness! Little wonder my friend's church grew. Joy, openness and overflowing generosity are so infectious.

Joy as Fullness

Few church leaders in recent memory embody the life in all its fullness as much as Pope Francis. He radiates it. A large lump appears in my throat when I read about him engaging with ordinary people with the love of Christ. Like pregnant Anna Romano, who was unaware that her boyfriend was already married. He left her when she

"At the end of the day it is not so much great faith in God as faith in a great God that matters."

Bishop Bill Flagg

refused to have an abortion. The local Priest then refused to baptise her child. Anna wrote to Pope Francis in desperation to ask for his advice. He called her out of the blue, and told her: *"If you can't find anyone to baptise your child - there's always me."*

In his book, *The Joy of the Gospel,* Pope Francis challenges us to rediscover the pure joy of knowing Jesus. It's that simple joy that will become so infectious and irresistible to those around us, he says. It's the key to our fullness.

Pope Francis writes: *'Whenever our interior life becomes caught up in its own interests and concerns, there is no longer room for others, no place for the poor. God's voice is no longer heard, the quiet joy of his love is no longer felt, and the desire to do good fades ... Many fall prey to it, and end up resentful, angry and listless. That is no way to live a dignified and fulfilled life; it is not God's will for us, nor is it the life in the Spirit which has its source in the heart of the risen Christ.'*

To put it another way, rediscovering the joy of knowing and being intimate with Christ generates a kind of spiritual patronus. A light that protects us from our Murdstonian tendencies, wards away the Dementors, and leads the way for others to meet with him.

So may each one of us be encouraged and freshly inspired to live fuller lives of joyful generosity. In the words of Apostle Paul from Romans 15: *'May the God of hope fill you with all joy and peace in believing, so that you may abound in hope by the power of the Holy Spirit.'*

You may like to go round the group and say those words to the person next to you as a way of affirming and blessing them. We all need to learn to channel our inner Peggotty!

"I did not know before my son told me that human beings are the only species that cries. There are complex chemical explanations why tears are a beneficial release of pent-up feelings, both physically and emotionally – the spiritual equivalent, you might say, of going to the gym … The poet Andrew Motion is not alone in testifying that he weeps more easily as he grows older. Film-maker Richard Curtis adds that advancing age invokes tears less at the 'sad and serious things in our lives' than at 'a tale of something good, some gracious or loving piece of behaviour'."

Anthony Holden, writer

Questions for Groups

YOU DON'T HAVE TO ANSWER ALL THE QUESTIONS!!

You can use some of your own if you prefer.

You should find that most of the questions refer to something either in the course booklet or on the audio (CD or download).

1. **Track 14 of the audio/transcript:** Discuss whether you think you're an introvert or an extrovert.
2. **Track 16:** Which of the nine fruits of the Spirit on p. 9 do you find most natural to live out - and which do you find the most elusive?
3. **Track 18:** Do you know people like the Murdstones? What sort of situation brings out the Murdstone tendencies in you?
4. **Tracks 19 & 20:** Who are the Peggotty people in your lives? What Christ-like qualities do you see in them?
5. **Read John 12 or hear it on track 13:** What are your immediate reactions to this passage in relation to life in all its fullness?
6. **Read John 3.16:** Share if you wish an experience of extravagant love in your life.
7. **Read John 12 or hear it on track 13:** What is your reaction to the way Jesus deals with Judas? How do you handle things when negative people seek to pull you down?
8. **Track 21:** Bill says church should be like your kitchen. Do you agree? Do you have any examples of Peggotty-type churches?
9. **Re-visit 'Joy as Fullness' on p. 13:** What is your view about Pope Francis' reaction to Anna Romano - the unmarried girl with a baby?
10. **Track 22:** Christ-like joy is one of the keys to living the 'full' life? Jot down some first steps to making changes towards this e.g. greeting a neighbour with a smile.
11. Do you agree with Anthony Holden's words in the box on p. 14? What would bring you more joy today?

"I would draw a distinction between being an optimist and being a hopeful person. I don't know that I think there's a lot of reason to be optimistic, but I am a person who tries to live hopefully. That is the gospel message. And I do know a lot of people who have none of our insurances, none of our padding, who still live with great hope."

Revd Kathy Galloway

Session 3: *Rotten or ripe?*

Read Luke 22.39-46

Back in my days as a local press newshound, I saw the world at its best, at its worst, and certainly at its weirdest. You really couldn't make it up. I once reported on a gentleman who was refused a bottle of his favourite sherry at the supermarket checkout until he could prove his age. He was 87!

My favourite story was one I wrote about an unforgettable Yorkshire terrier called Ratty. His owner was baffled that he kept disappearing from the family farm most afternoons. One day he followed Ratty, to solve the mystery.

It turns out this amazing little dog was hopping onto a Number 10 bus at a stop outside the farm, and disembarking a mile down the road. He would then cross the busy main road to the Black Bull pub, where a barmaid showered him with doggy treats. After a few hours rest, Ratty would catch another bus back to the farm and cross the road again!

I wrote about a lot of bad news too. The paper was full of it every day. The fatal crashes, the house fires, the brutal robberies and the tragic cot deaths. I once had the grim task of reporting on a quadruple murder investigation. The newsroom was a stark daily reminder of how glorious and horrible the world could sometimes be.

Amid a cruel world

As we continue our journey reflecting on Christ's offer of 'life in all its fullness', we'll consider in this session how this is possible amid the reality of such a messy, unpredictable and often cruel world.

David Attenborough (our muse from Session 1) said he has often been chastised by viewers for not giving God enough credit for the beauty of nature. *"They always quote orchids and hummingbirds and butterflies and roses,"* he said, *"but I always have to think too of a little boy sitting on the banks of a river in west Africa, who has a worm boring through his eyeball, turning him blind before he's five years old. And I reply and say, 'Well, presumably the God you speak about created the worm as well.'"*

It's a fair point. God's world can be beautiful and bleak. Yet Jesus doesn't caveat his offer of fullness just for those times when our lives are full of butterflies and roses. It must also apply to the worm-eaten times.

> "For most of the time, our faith presents us with not soothing comfort, but with probing, life-enhancing challenge."
>
> *Revd Preb. Gillean Craig*

The Bible never whitewashes life's harsh realities. Far from it. Take a book like Ecclesiastes, surely one of the most earthy, compelling and contradictory in the entire canon. One scholar says it is a profoundly religious book because it seeks to 'grapple with reality'. In Ecclesiastes 3, the narrator lays it on the line. *'There is a time for everything ...a time to be born and a time to die ... a time to weep and a time to laugh, a time to mourn and a time to dance ...'*

The gift of poetry

In recent years I've found poetry to be a profound gift in helping me to grapple with these realities. The late Irish poet and Nobel Prize winner, Seamus Heaney, is one of my favourites. I suspect Attenborough would approve of Heaney's early work, as it takes its inspiration from both the beauty and the horror of the natural world. The flowers and the worms. No more so than in his poem *Blackberry-Picking.*

The first half of the poem describes the simple joy of blackberries ripening into blossom. It paints a beautiful word-picture of summer freshness, and the fruitfulness of new life in blossom. Heaney describes the first tantalising blackberry coming into season, its sweet flesh *'Like thickened wine'.* Pickers are compelled to go out to the hedgerows to fill cans and jam pots with the delicious fruit. Mouths and fingers become sticky and juice-stained.

Many of us have wonderful memories of those ripe blackberry moments in our journey with God. Those times - however fleeting - when everything just made sense and clicked into place. When we experienced a palpable sense of Christ's fullness bubbling up within us. When we felt our prayers and praises being heard in a fresh, intimate way - as if Christ was sitting right beside us. When our faith felt like a gloriously simple gift.

Retreating to progress

My own times of spiritual ripeness have always been an unexpected delight. I particularly remember my first silent retreat, not long before I was ordained. I was dreading being forced to stay quiet for three days! To my shame, I hatched a plan with a similarly extroverted roommate to sneak off to the pub one night so we could offload loudly over crisps and ale. God had other ideas, though.

That afternoon I'd gone for a walk in the grounds of the retreat house. Walking into a clearing beside a stream, I was suddenly overcome by an acute sense of God's presence. I was so aware of him in the wonder of creation all around me. In the sound of the flowing water, in the light rustle of the trees. I didn't see

> "All of man's misery comes from his incapacity to sit alone in an empty quiet room."
>
> *Blaise Pascal, theologian*

> "God must have been on holiday."
> *Samuel Willenberg, Holocaust survivor*

any visions or hear any voices. No burning bushes confronted me. I just knew without doubt in that moment that Christ was with me - and all was well. I've seldom felt so loved and called. I must have scared a few squirrels as I shouted out prayers of thanks and recited some lines from my favourite Psalms. Then I skipped back to join the others at the house for a silent meal of sausages and mash. I cancelled our clandestine pub visit.

The great spiritual mystic St Ignatius called these ripe spiritual periods, times of 'consolation'. They seem to come to us at particular seasons and seldom last for any length of time. Just like the pleasure of eating a delicious blackberry, they are a gift to us. It's important we enjoy and savour them as such.

Faith in the face of brokenness

I had a bruising conversation the other day with a guy grieving the death of his parents. He was incredulous that I could even entertain the idea of a faith in God. "You don't *really* believe do you, Matt?" he raged. "How can you? I held both my parents' hands as they died. They were in so much pain. It was horrible. How can there be a God who would let that happen? There's just nothing!" Admittedly, I had no easy answers for this man. The encounter was another stark reminder of just how broken and unfair the world can be at times.

In the second half of Heaney's *Blackberry-Picking* poem, he writes of storing away the fresh blackberries and returning to them some time later. There's a hopeful expectation that they will be just as deliciously ripe as when first left. In reality though, he's distressed to find they've become furry, fungus-ridden and foul-smelling. The blackberries have rotted. He writes, *'Each year I hoped they'd keep, knew they would not.'* You can read the whole brilliant poem in Heaney's first book of poetry *Death of a Naturalist* (and many other subsequent collections.)

Our lives are sometimes soured and spoiled like those blackberries. Sometimes it's of our own making. We spoil and sour the world around us because of our mistakes, selfishness or harsh treatment of others. Who amongst us hasn't felt the heavy weight of being a flawed human being? Often, of course, despite our hopes and best laid plans, despite our most fervent, heartfelt prayers, things happen out of our control. Our lives fall foul of the harsh treatment of others, illness strikes, we lose our job, or a loved one dies suddenly.

No immunity for Christians

One of the most painful realisations we can have as Christians is that we are not immune from bad things happening to us. We all have our own examples.

For my family most recently, it was when my wife was struck down with a condition called 'ice pick headaches'. They can suddenly strike for no apparent reason. Sufferers are consumed by an intense pain that feels like an ice pick has been stabbed into their eyeball. All was well prior to this happening. We were in 'summer blackberry picking season' as a family. The headaches rotted our world for months until eventually the condition was successfully treated. Admittedly, we had some harsh words for God. Where was he? Why was this happening? Why didn't he answer our prayers? What had happened to our life in all its fullness?

Looking back now, I see how much my wife and I learnt during that awful time: about ourselves, about our love for each other, about our faith in Christ. There were no miraculous healings or angelic visitations. Just a gruelling period of clinging on. Many of us at such times experience that great Christian paradox: that when we are weak, we are strong. Perhaps this is the key to living in Christ's fullness when all seems lost and broken.

Sharing the pain

It's important to remember that Jesus was fully immersed in our 'blackberry world'. He absolutely identifies with our pain and despair. Few Gospel scenes illustrate this more than Luke 22.

We know that the Garden of Gethsemane, situated at the foot of the Mount of Olives, was a special place for Jesus. A place of prayerful intimacy with his father. A place of refreshment and renewal. A place of spiritual ripeness. He now returns there to face down the rot. To plead for deliverance from the impending horrors of Calvary's cross. *'Father if you are willing, remove this cup from me,'* he cries out in verse 42. Luke records that such was Jesus' anguish, such was the depth of his prayer, that *'his sweat was like drops of blood falling to the ground.'*

How often have we cried out to God in such a way when life has become unbearable? So often it feels like he doesn't hear us. Our prayers seem to go unheard – or unanswered. In Gethsemane, Christ did not get the answer he wanted. The cup was not taken from him. Yet God gave him the strength to drink from it.

In contrast to those periods of consolation in our spiritual lives, St Ignatius calls our 'Gethsemane' periods, times of 'desolation'. He believed that clinging to Christ at such times grows us to a deeper understanding of what it means to be a disciple and of living in his fullness.

> "Religions, all of them, are coping strategies. They're people trying to find explanations, rationalise their existences, deal with pain, and work out how to live."
> *Cathy Rentzenbrink, author*

> "I will never leave thee nor forsake thee. Jesus Christ the same yesterday, today and forever. Tested, tried and proved. (Heb, 13:5 &8)"
>
> *Opening entry (1916) in WWI field notebook of Pte Albert Edwin Evanson*

There's always a psalm

King David knew all about clinging. He was a man after God's *'own heart'*, 1 Samuel says. So much trust was put in him. So much was achieved by him in God's name.

However, David knew more than most what it meant to find spiritual strength out of his own human weakness. He wrote many, if not all, of the psalms, and those that he most likely wrote read like his personal diary entries on the blackberry life in all its ripeness and rot. It's worth pausing to reflect on his words in Psalm 63. It's a clinging prayer. A Gethsemane moment. David chooses to bring God into all his loneliness and fear. I'm sure many of us can identify with his words. He writes:

'You, God, are my God,
earnestly I seek you;
I thirst for you,
my whole being longs for you,
in a dry and parched land
where there is no water ...

On my bed I remember you;

I think of you through the watches of the night.

Because you are my help,

I sing in the shadow of your wings.

I cling to you;

your right hand upholds me.'

Drifting away

I always find it particularly sad in church life when people drift away during times of pain and distress. They let go rather than cling on. Sometimes it's because of an unconscious feeling that they will be thought less of, or that they have somehow let people down.

I once visited a lady who hadn't been to church for some weeks. It turns out there had been a family crisis. "I couldn't let you all see me like this," she sobbed. "I'll be back when things get better." I reassured her that church works the other way round. Drawing strength and comfort from the love of God's people in our rotten times is what defines the essence and beauty of a healthy Christian community. The simple love and care of others is often what keeps us living in the fullness of Christ.

In his poem *Days*, Philip Larkin offers us a stark reminder that whether we like it or not, we can't live anywhere but in days. Every morning - until our last breath - we enter into a new one. We can't predict what will happen. We don't know what story will be written. Larkin writes that days are *'to be happy in'* (which was ironic, given he could be such a cynical curmudgeon!).

> "It is not my ability, but my response to God's ability, that counts."
>
> *Corrie Ten Boom*

However I'm learning that, as followers of Christ, our days are to be 'full' in. Trusting Jesus will not always make our lives happy - but it will make them full. Full on the good days and the bad days, the easy days and the hard days, and yes, on the ripe days and the rotten days. His love will never fail us.

Coming home

It's important that as followers of Christ we never waste any of our days: to seek to bring a taste of God's Kingdom to our imperfect world; to be alert and ready for that day of days when Christ will return to restore all the 'blackberries' as they were created to be.

Please let me encourage you to finish the session by reciting this extract from the Old Testament scholar Walter Brueggemann's refreshingly honest 'clinging' prayer:

'In our secret yearnings
we wait for your coming,
and in our grinding despair
we doubt that you will ...
Give us the grace and the impatience
to wait for your coming to the bottom of our toes,
to the edges of our fingertips ...
Come in your power
and come in your weakness
in any case
and make all things new.
Amen.'

> "Of course it's instinctive for us to feel that what happens to us is ordained by God, and many religious writers say this. And I know that sometimes, when people's hearts are broken with sorrow, the one thing they can cling to is: well, it's God's will. And yet, of course, this is not so, because God never wants bad things to happen to us. It's the last thing he wants, for us to suffer. He wants us to be happy. What God wants is to be with us in what we suffer... And I think the same is true of the good things. God's *delighted* that we have a summer day. He's *delighted* that our headache has gone. He grieves *with* us when our parents die. And the sad thing is that he's there with his arms around us in sorrow - and people just don't see him. It would be nonsense to even think of blaming God, when he hung on the cross for us. Can you imagine Jesus sending us bad things when he was alive? And yet what Jesus does is what the Father does. That is the image of God. And it was never in his heart that people should ever suffer. "
>
> *Sr Wendy Beckett,* (York Course: Praise Him)

Questions for Groups

YOU DON'T HAVE TO ANSWER ALL THE QUESTIONS!!

You can use some of your own if you prefer.

You should find that most of the questions refer to something either in the course booklet or on the audio (CD or download).

1. What good, bad, or amusing news has caught your eye in the media recently?
2. **Re-visit 'Amid a cruel world' on p. 16 and track 25 of the audio/transcript:** What is your reaction to David Attenborough's words?
3. **Read Ecclesiastes 3.1-8:** Discuss Matt's assertion that 'the Bible never whitewashes life's harsh realities'.
4. **Re-visit 'The gift of poetry' on p. 17:** Share a time when you've experienced spiritual ripeness. Has the wonder of creation ever come alive to you?
5. **Read Matthew 11.28-30 and track 27:** Can you share a difficult time in your life when 'your blackberries felt rotten'? What brought you comfort? What impact did it have on your faith?
6. **Re-visit 'Retreating to progress' on p. 17 and track 28:** Have you ever been on a silent retreat? If so, how did you find it? If not, can you see the point of it?
7. **Read Luke 22 and re-visit 'Sharing the pain' on p. 19:** Are you willing to share a 'Gethsemane moment' where you felt your prayer was unheard – or not answered as you had hoped?
8. **Re-read the extract from Psalm 63 on p. 20 and track 30:** Discuss the apparent contradiction of a brutal world and a God of love. Why isn't there immunity from suffering for believers?
9. **Track 31 and Cathy Rentzenbrink's words on p. 19:** Does it help you to know that Jesus shares our pain?
10. **Tracks 32 & 33:** How can our church communities help people more effectively when life goes wrong?
11. **Matt writes on p. 20 that 'the simple love and care of others is often what keeps us living in the fullness of Christ':** Does this help you when times are hard?

"We have become used to the idea that silence is dead time, time that should be filled at all costs. We try to interrupt the silence – if there is no exterior noise – by making plans inside our heads or just holding an internal conversation with ourselves. Using silence – a silence that is God channelled – so that God may truly change us is a far more demanding and certainly scarier occupation."

Archbishop Richard Armagh

Session 4: *Desert or Oasis?*

Read: John 4.4-30, 39-42

I can only remember two things from my Religious Education lessons at secondary school. (I'll never become Archbishop of Canterbury at this rate!) The first is to recite the names of the twelve disciples at breakneck speed, in this order: 'Peter, Andrew, James, John, Philip, Bartholomew, Thomas, Matthew, James, Jude, Simon, Judas.'

Mr Sargent and the cool drink

The second thing is a lovely story our long-suffering teacher Mr Sargent once told us in a lesson. He reminisced about going on a long trek with his close friend one baking hot summer's day. They'd walked for hours before collapsing panting and exhausted by a stream. Their water supplies had run low and their mouths were dry. "What's the one thing in the world you'd like right now?" Mr Sargent's friend asked him a bit later, as they melted in the heat. "A nice, cold bottle of beer," Mr Sargent replied without hesitation. His friend disappeared towards the stream, and, returning, placed a bottle of cold beer into Mr Sargent's hand. "Your wish is my command!"

> "We are thirsty for God. He is to be found, not in the shadowy creations of men, but in the concrete historical figure of Jesus of Nazareth."
>
> *Revd Dr John Polkinghorne*

I remember my teacher describing what it was like to have his thirst quenched by that cold drink. How it revived him and cheered him. How warm he felt towards his friend for making such a kind, thoughtful, and surprising gesture. Admittedly, my 15-year-old self was also a bit taken aback that my crusty RE teacher drank beer with his mates! For a few minutes, Mr Sargent was actually cool.

I mention this because it reminded me that a huge factor in living in the fullness of Christ - maybe the key to it all - is inviting God's Spirit to revive our inner places. To drink deeply of his living water. It's how we stay full. And, like Mr Sargent's friend, it's how we are able to share Christ's fullness with others. So, in this last session, we're thinking about the Holy Spirit and the difference between living our spiritual lives in the desert or the oasis.

Living on Empty

If we're honest, so many of us live Saharan-like Christian lives.

We often walk with God in a permanently parched state. We survive on little sips. Scrabble around blindly in the sun. Lose the sense of who we are in Christ and where we are going. And that's just the vicars!

Of course, there are often good reasons for being sucked dry and living on empty. Remember the hummingbirds, the Murdstones and the blackberries from the previous sessions? Nevertheless, I know from personal experience that sometimes we can simply grow stale and complacent. Lazy, even. If we're not careful, the familiarity of our journey with God can breed a kind of unconscious contempt.

Drawing from the deep well

Of course deserts, wildernesses, times of 'desolation' - as we touched on in the last session - are often those periods when we learn the most about our need for God. They can be times to toughen up and wise up. Yet for Jesus there came a point - when he came out of the wilderness after 40 days - where angels helped to restore and refresh him for the days ahead. He daily drew strength from his father in heaven.

The 97th Archbishop of York, Dr John Sentamu, is fond of reminding the Church that our best laid plans and human efforts are in vain unless we continually draw from the deep well of the Holy Spirit.

Reflecting on Christ's invitation in John 7.37-38, Archdeacon John Kiddle writes: '*If you are thirsty, Jesus says, come to me and drink. Receive the Spirit who, like a river of living water, is the one who draws us and all the world into relationship with God. As it was for Jesus so it can be for us.*'

The obvious question then, is why do we so often - spiritually speaking - find ourselves bedouin-like in waterless, desert landscapes desperate for a drink?

Perhaps one reason is an awkwardness, a hesitancy or even a fear over 'receiving the Holy Spirit'. He is the person of the Holy Trinity that people often find most difficult, confusing or elusive. Some of the Spirit's wilder descriptions, manifestations and mysteries, documented in the New Testament and replicated in many charismatic-type churches today, can prove too much for some people.

Asking and receiving

Unusually, for such a loud extrovert, when it comes to the Holy Spirit I retreat into my shell. I tend to receive from him in a quiet, reserved way. Some of my friends are far more public. Does it matter? I don't think so. The important part is the asking and receiving. The Holy Spirit is our gift to draw from - regardless

> "God isn't looking for people of great faith, but for individuals ready to follow him."
>
> *James Hudson Taylor, Christian missionary*

> "Evangelisation is a process of bringing the gospel to people where they are, not where you would like them to be ... When the gospel reaches a people where they are, their response to the gospel is the church in a new place."
>
> *Bishop Vincent Donovan*

of character, style or particular worship preference. We all need his help, comfort and strength - lots of it. It's my experience that we don't get very far in our faith journey without him. He makes all the difference.

One former colleague can testify to that. He described a profound experience he had on retreat recently. By his own admission, he was drained spiritually up to that point. Existing in the desert. The demands of a busy parish and a major church building project had taken its toll. He was worn out, stressed out and probably on the cusp of burn-out.

One afternoon in a quiet chapel he found his oasis. Kneeling at the font, as the sound of the water gently stirred, he poured out to God all his fears, stresses and doubts. He asked the Holy Spirit to fill him. To restore and revive him. To calm the storm raging within. In the quiet beauty of that chapel he was stilled and filled afresh. He came back a different man.

No point in waiting

An important lesson from this story is not to leave it so long. Too often we wait until we're struggling in the desert before we turn to the Spirit to slake our thirst.

The late spiritual renewal leader, David Watson, made it his life's mission to lead people to the water. He wrote: *'When Paul wrote "Be filled with the Spirit", the tense he used implied that we should go on being filled with the Spirit. It should be a continuous, daily, ever-fresh renewing. The Holy Spirit comes to guide you into God's perfect will for your life, and to fill your heart every day with the love of God - a love to be shared with others.'*

Searching

I have an unhealthy obsession with the Manchester rock band *Oasis*. I still horde a treasured collection of their t-shirts, badges and key-rings - like some kind of teenage teenybopper. Something about their songs, their look, and the northern swagger of the Gallagher brothers has always resonated with me. At a concert in Liverpool - just weeks before I got ordained - I lost leave of my senses and attempted my first crowd surf. Hoisted high onto the sea of raised arms I was transported over the heads towards Liam Gallagher on stage. For a few fleeting moments I was in rock heaven. That was until I was dumped headfirst into the security pit and nearly broke my neck! There's a sermon there somewhere.

> "I don't know why we are here, but I'm pretty sure it is not in order to enjoy ourselves."
>
> *Ludwig Wittgenstein, philosopher*

With song titles like *Cigarettes and Alcohol, Rock and Roll Star* and *Champagne Supernova,* the music of Oasis may appear far from deep or spiritual. However I now see that much of their early material is actually about lost-ness: a yearning for a fuller life. For me, they are desert songs.

Ironically, Oasis seemed to be searching for an oasis. When their career went supersonic they thought they'd found it. Becoming one of the world's biggest bands, they indulged in all the hedonistic trappings of success, money and fame. Yet it doesn't seem to have been enough. Noel Gallagher penned songs not of triumph or fulfilment, but regret and lament. *Who Put The Weight Of the World On My Shoulders?* and *Where Did It All Go Wrong?* are two such examples.

The band has since disbanded acrimoniously. I suspect their search goes on though. The Gallagher brothers are not alone. Many people are searching for an oasis. They long to know whether God is real and, if so, what practical difference he might make. The Psalmist articulates it like this: *'My soul thirsts for God, for the living God. Where can I go and meet with God?'*

Good news to share

I've discovered that our conversations, invitations and example are so often the way thirsty people find refreshment in God. South African theologian David Bosch wrote that: *'Christians find their true identity when they are involved in mission, in communicating to others a new way of life ... in committing themselves to the liberation and salvation of others.'* We have good news to share!

Of course how we do that is the trickier question, but seeing how Jesus did it has got to be the best way to follow. As far as I can tell, Jesus got alongside people in a spirit of love and compassion. He gently challenged them to 'come and see', 'come and drink' and 'come and be filled'. He never forced, or pressured or cajoled - but he always invited.

Thirsty searchers

Throughout the Gospels, from Nicodemus to Zacchaeus, Jesus is always looking for the thirsty searchers. His encounter with the Samaritan woman at the well in John 4.7-30 is a revealing example. Married five times, the woman was clearly carrying the baggage and burdens of a messy life. With care and compassion, Jesus helps her to think about the difference between the world's desert offerings and God's abundant oasis.

'Everyone who drinks this water will be thirsty again,' Jesus tells her. Then,

in one of the most powerful, life-changing statements in the entire Gospels, he says: *'Anyone who drinks the water I give will never thirst - not ever. The water I give will be an artesian spring within, gushing fountains of endless life.'* [The Message Version.]

When the woman's heart had been opened to this promise, she felt immediately compelled to pass the 'living water' bottle around town! To give her neighbours the chance to taste it for themselves. The result? Verse 39: *'Many of the Samaritans from that town believed in him because of the woman's testimony.'*

For me this is the essence of evangelism - a word much maligned and misunderstood in recent years, but which literally means sharing the good news. In essence we drink of the living water. We are filled. We invite others to drink.

Doorman to choir-man

Kenny was someone I plucked up the courage to invite a few years ago. He was a doorman providing security at a real ale festival held in our church in Hull. Chatting to him that week, I realised that he was more interested in the things of the spirit than in the glasses of beer. He was lost and searching. To my encouragement to come to our Sunday service, he responded: "Am I really allowed to come?" It broke my heart. He didn't think he'd actually be allowed in!

> "Somebody should tell us, right at the start of our lives, that we are dying. Then we might live life to the limit, every minute, of every day."
>
> *Pope Paul VI*

Kenny did turn up in the end. And Christ met with him in a special way. Kenny has now swapped his black suit and earpiece for a red robe, frilly cuffs and an outrageous collar … Kenny has joined the church choir! When asked later what difference his faith had made, he replied: "It's given me new life. New friends. It's given me belief that there's always someone there to help you. It's helping me be a better man than I used to be."

A life lived in the fullness of Christ, then, is always a life we share with others. There's enormous power in a simple invitation. Just ask Kenny.

Dying of thirst in the Gobi Desert

To draw this session to a close, I want to finish with a real-life account of the Swedish explorer called Sven Hedin who, during a failed expedition in 1895, was stranded in the Gobi Desert and dying of thirst. It perhaps sums up what we've been thinking about in this session. It spoke to me about my own spiritual journey. I hope it speaks to you.

'I had not strength enough to follow the others. They had left me. The horrible

desert extended in all directions. The sun was burning and blinding; there was not a breath of air ... I did not want to die: I would not die in this miserable, sandy desert! I could run, walk, crawl on my hands and feet ... I had to find water! Kasim [a member of the expedition party who was with Sven] *grabbed my arm and pointed downwards at the sand. There were distinct tracks of human beings!*

[After more torturous days of trekking, lost, delirious and close to death, Sven finds himself alone on the edge of what he thought was a dry river bed …] *'Suddenly I started and stopped short. A water-bird, a wild duck or goose, rose on whirring wings and I heard a splash. The next moment, I stood on the edge of a pool, seventy feet long and fifteen feet wide! ... I thanked God for my miraculous deliverance ...Then I drank, and drank again. I drank without restraint. The water was cold, clear as crystal, and sweet as the best spring-water. And then I drank again. My dried-up body absorbed the moisture like a sponge ... I had a feeling of well-being and comfort.'*

> "Believing in the resurrection can and should transform not only how we view the world, but how we live in it. We should become people in whom others can see new life."
>
> *Paula Gooder, theologian*

[Feeling revived, Sven then went to find and rescue Kasim.] *'Upon seeing me, Kasim whispered: "I am dying!" "Will you have some water?" I asked, letting him hear the splashing sound. He lifted it to his lips and emptied it to the last drop.*

Jesus said: *'I have come so that you may have life and have it to the full.'* Let me encourage you to drink in the fullness of Christ without restraint. To drink and drink again! And then to ask others: 'Will you have some?'

God bless. Stay full!

> "It's interesting that 67% of non-Christians know a Christian, but only 1% know a vicar. Leaving everything to the clergy is therefore not an option … There's a distinction between what we do as 'gathered' church and 'sent' church. In other words, what we do when we gather together, usually on Sundays, should strengthen and equip us to make an impact for Christ on the world around us – the world we are part of when we are not in church.
>
> Mission is not about removing people from the world to seek refuge within the Church, but about releasing and empowering all God's people in order that the whole of creation might be transformed and restored in Christ."
>
> *Church of England's 2017 report* Setting God's people free

Questions for Groups

YOU DON'T HAVE TO ANSWER ALL THE QUESTIONS!!

You can use some of your own if you prefer.

You should find that most of the questions refer to something either in the course booklet or on the audio (CD or download).

1. Who was your favourite teacher and why?
2. **Re-visit 'Drawing from the deep well' on. p. 24 and track 36 of the audio/ transcript:** Do you thirst spiritually? Where is the well that you could - or do - drink from?
3. **Track 40:** Many people struggle with an understanding of the Holy Spirit. In what ways might 'being filled with the Spirit' be intimidating or awkward for some?
4. **Tracks 41 & 42:** What is your experience of the Holy Spirit? Can you share a time when you were filled? Or do you tend to receive from him in a quiet or private way?
5. **Re-visit 'Doorman to choir-man' on p. 27:** Kenny says his faith is 'helping me to be a better man that I used to be'. Is this a conversion?
6. **Read John 4.4-30,39 and track 43:** Do you struggle with the idea of evangelism – or with putting it into practice? What strikes you about Jesus' encounter with the Samaritan woman?
7. **Track 44:** Can you understand why some people think they're not allowed to come to church? How might we encourage them otherwise?
8. **Re-visit 'Dying of thirst in the Gobi Desert' on p. 27:** Which parts of Sven Hedin's journey resonate with where you are right now with God - or perhaps where you want to be?
9. How might God be speaking to you? What might he be challenging you to do - or to stop doing?
10. What have you learnt together about living in the fullness of Christ?

What next for your group?

You may like to meet again – perhaps over the new 5-session York Course written by Bishop Nick Baines: *Daring to see God now* on hearing, understanding and living 'the Good News of God' in today's world.

You may like to end this final session by saying together this Closing Prayer:

'Lord as you will,
Lord as you know.
Have mercy on us,
have mercy.'

A FOUR-SESSION COURSE

for discussion groups and individuals - suitable for Advent or any season

MATT WOODCOCK is a pioneer minister and mission enabler for the Diocese of York. He helps churches to grow. Matt was a former newspaper reporter for the York Evening Press. He is married and has twin 7-year-old daughters. His passions include hot curries, *Oasis*, reading, and the paintings of Caravaggio. Matt is a regular *Pause for Thought* contributor on Radio Two and author of *Becoming Reverend*.

SIMON STANLEY is a co-founder of *York Courses*, a Canon Emeritus of York Minster, and a former BBC producer/presenter ... Simon was also a regular *Pause for Thought* contributor - many years before Matt!

Four sessions:

Session 1: Hummingbird or Arctic Fox?
Session 2: Murdstone or Peggotty?
Session 3: Rotten or ripe?
Session 4: Desert or Oasis?

THE COURSE BOOKLET is written by Matt Woodcock. Each of the four sessions ends with a range of questions designed to stimulate lively group discussion. Ideally each group member should have a personal copy.

THE AUDIO contains a relaxed conversation between Matt Woodcock and Simon Stanley, exploring and expanding on topics raised in the course booklet, with contributions from churchgoers of different denominations.

THE COURSE TRANSCRIPT booklet is a complete record of the words spoken on the recorded material, and includes CD track numbers. Especially useful for group leaders as they prepare, it can also help group members to feel more confident about joining in the discussion; to catch up on missed sessions; and to go over the recorded material at leisure.

The audio material and course booklet work hand-in-hand with each other and both are essential in following the development of the themes raised in this course.

OUR WARM THANKS to Julie Skelton of Appletree Design Solutions for the design and digital downloads, and to Jerry Ibbotson for recording and producing the course audio.

York Courses · PO Box 343 · York
YO19 5YB UK · Tel : 01904 466516
email: courses@yorkcourses.co.uk

www.yorkcourses.co.uk

YORK COURSES

9 781909 107212

ISBN 978-1-909107-21-2